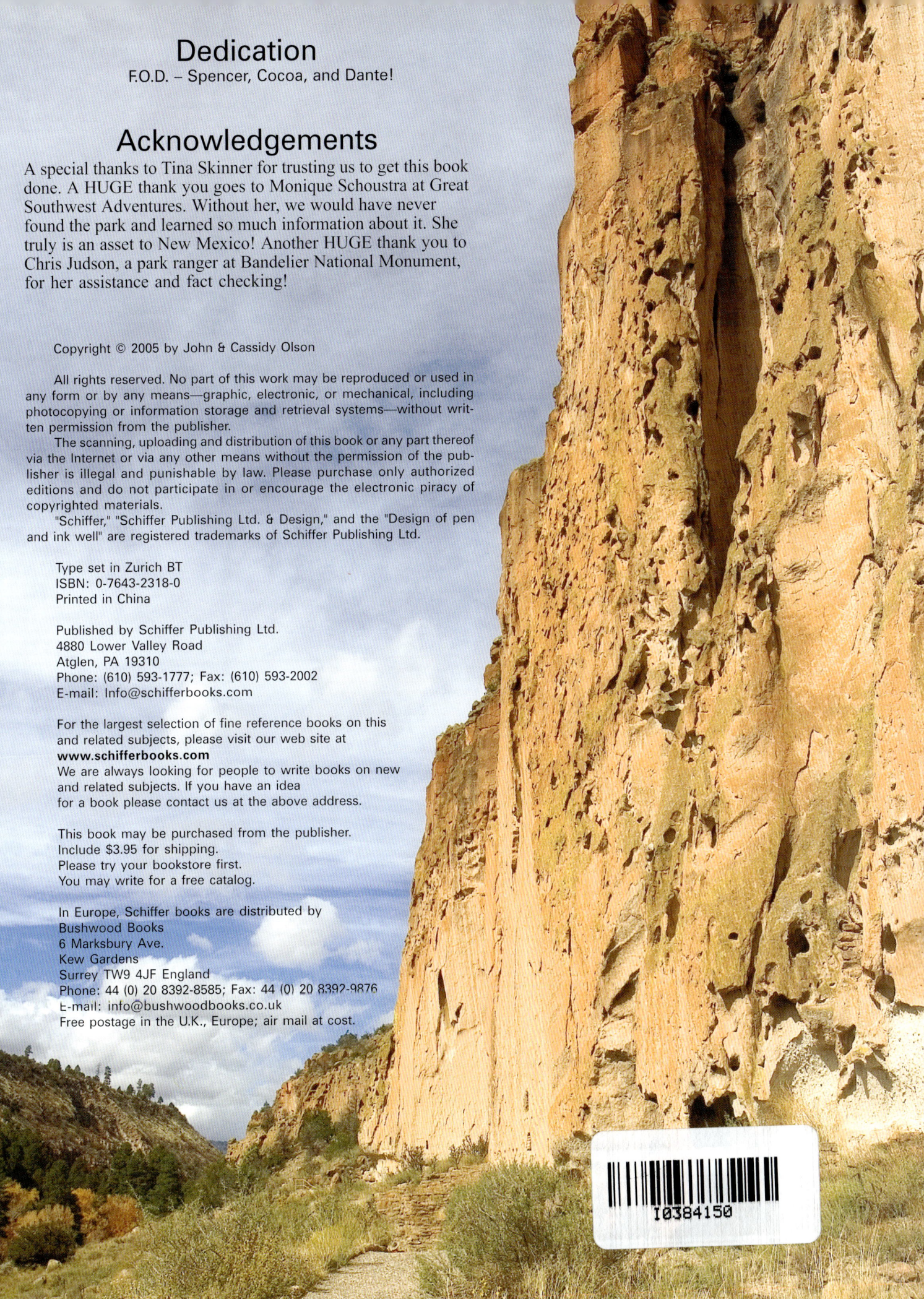

Dedication
F.O.D. – Spencer, Cocoa, and Dante!

Acknowledgements
A special thanks to Tina Skinner for trusting us to get this book done. A HUGE thank you goes to Monique Schoustra at Great Southwest Adventures. Without her, we would have never found the park and learned so much information about it. She truly is an asset to New Mexico! Another HUGE thank you to Chris Judson, a park ranger at Bandelier National Monument, for her assistance and fact checking!

Copyright © 2005 by John & Cassidy Olson

All rights reserved. No part of this work may be reproduced or used in any form or by any means—graphic, electronic, or mechanical, including photocopying or information storage and retrieval systems—without written permission from the publisher.

The scanning, uploading and distribution of this book or any part thereof via the Internet or via any other means without the permission of the publisher is illegal and punishable by law. Please purchase only authorized editions and do not participate in or encourage the electronic piracy of copyrighted materials.

"Schiffer," "Schiffer Publishing Ltd. & Design," and the "Design of pen and ink well" are registered trademarks of Schiffer Publishing Ltd.

Type set in Zurich BT
ISBN: 0-7643-2318-0
Printed in China

Published by Schiffer Publishing Ltd.
4880 Lower Valley Road
Atglen, PA 19310
Phone: (610) 593-1777; Fax: (610) 593-2002
E-mail: Info@schifferbooks.com

For the largest selection of fine reference books on this and related subjects, please visit our web site at
www.schifferbooks.com
We are always looking for people to write books on new and related subjects. If you have an idea for a book please contact us at the above address.

This book may be purchased from the publisher.
Include $3.95 for shipping.
Please try your bookstore first.
You may write for a free catalog.

In Europe, Schiffer books are distributed by
Bushwood Books
6 Marksbury Ave.
Kew Gardens
Surrey TW9 4JF England
Phone: 44 (0) 20 8392-8585; Fax: 44 (0) 20 8392-9876
E-mail: info@bushwoodbooks.co.uk
Free postage in the U.K., Europe; air mail at cost.

One and a half million years ago, enormous ash and debris flows covered the land now known as Bandelier National Monument. The Jemez Mountains were created, and surface water and wind began to wear away areas of ash, creating cliffs and valleys. Erosion created the "finger mesas" that come out from the mountains. In between two of these "finger mesas" is Frijoles Canyon, ancestral home to many Pueblos.

Bandelier National Monument
Home of the Ancestral Pueblo People

John and Cassidy Olson
Photography by Olson Photographic LLC

4880 Lower Valley Road, Atglen, PA 19310 USA

Introduction

Bandelier National Monument is located near Los Alamos, New Mexico. The history of the area is still unfolding. Current day Bandelier National Monument is surrounded by the Jemez Mountains. Volcanic activity in the Jemez Volcanic field began millions of years ago. About 1.5 million years ago, there was an eruption at least 600 times as powerful as the 1980 eruption of Mount St. Helens. It covered hundreds of square miles with airborne ash and pyroclastic flows. These ashflows formed the Pajarito Plateau. The volcano collapsed in on itself, creating a huge caldera now known as the Valles Caldera. Ash on the edges of flows cooled quickly, becoming a soft, crumbly rock called tuff, while ash in the interior of flows cooled more slowly (in some cases, it may have taken many years) making welded tuff, which is much harder. In several areas the volcano produced obsidian, or volcanic glass. Water and time wore away parts of the ash to create cliffs and Frijoles Canyon. The Rito de los Frijoles (Little Bean Creek) still flows today.

Thousands of years ago, long before the arrival of the Spanish in the area, nomadic hunters and gatherers lived throughout the Four Corners area. Since they and their descendants, the Ancestral Pueblo people, left no written language, archeologists are still working to piece together their history and timeline. The time span of the Pueblo people and their ancestors is, at the shortest, 15,000 years, and is thus deserving of the attention that is paid to it. The lineage has been effectively traced back to the Paleoindian people of the Americas and further back still to the people who came from the Old World via the Bering Land Bridge. By the birth of Jesus, people were beginning to settle into permanent villages, making their living by farming. In the early 1900s, some archeologists believed that the Ancestral Pueblo people had simply disappeared, leaving only their villages of stone homes as lasting evidence that they even existed. Others felt they had left in search of greener pastures. The Pueblo people knew there wasn't any real mystery about where their ancestors had gone – their grandparents were living right next door. Charting the progress of the Ancestral Pueblo people shows them moving progressively south as the years rolled by. The movement was probably precipitated by exhaustion of local materials and rainfall, or the lack thereof. As an area either had its natural resources depleted or the rainfall changed drastically for the worse, people

Existing holes in the cliffs were hollowed out and used as living space and storage. The dwellings were accessible by ladders and often had stone rooms in front of them.

packed up and left. By the year 500, groups of Ancestral Pueblo people were in present-day Utah and Colorado. By 700, they were on the Colorado Plateau and in the northern Rio Grande basin of New Mexico. Two famous and important settlement areas are the archeological sites now known as Chaco Canyon and Mesa Verde. While each was a distinctly different group of Ancestral Pueblo people, they both played a part in the history of the people who would later live in Bandelier. Chaco Canyon prospered for a long time, but the people were leaving by the 1100s. At Mesa Verde, the exodus occurred in the late 1200s. Historically, biologically and archeologically speaking, no one knows for sure why those two communities ultimately failed. At Mesa Verde, there was a drought for almost thirty years, ending in 1299, but tree rings show that there had been other, more severe droughts earlier in their time there. A change in housing patterns suggests trouble or unrest, in that many of the people moved from mesa-top villages to the famous cliff dwellings just within the final century of habitation. Drought was almost certainly not the whole story of why the people left the formerly thriving trade and ceremonial center now called Chaco Canyon in the 1100s. In both, homes were extremely well built, were very modern for the time, and appear to have been made for a large thriving community. By 1100, the area now known as Bandelier National Monument began to increase in population. If part of the increase was due to people who had formerly lived in Chaco Canyon, they must have felt that they had found their paradise. In Frijoles Canyon, there was a year-round stream. Mesa tops offered wide spaces for farming. Wood and wildlife were available. People had lived in Bandelier for thousands of years, but the heyday of the Ancestral Pueblo people there was from the early 1100s to the mid-1500s.

Very early in the history of people in the Southwest, caves must have served as shelter and temporary homes, especially during winter months. The early hunters and gatherers in the Bandelier area left very little trace of their passing, only a few distinctive projectile points; we have no evidence of their taste in shelters. When people in the area began choosing to settle down, at first villages were small. By the 1300s, archeologists find evidence of "aggregation" – groups moving together into large villages such as the community in Frijoles Canyon, possibly for protection.

Perhaps the growing population in the 1100s brought the need for change. Natural holes in the cliffs of Frijoles Canyon had probably been used to some extent for millennia, but now people carved them into convenient shapes for use as living and storage areas. They dug out spaces in the cliffs to anchor beams to be supports for roofs and floors, and built stone homes along the base of the cliffs. The cave rooms (known as cavates) served as back rooms for living or storage. Niches were sometimes carved inside the caves for storage. A circular village called *Tyuonyi* was built on the floor of Frijoles Canyon for housing and food storage. It was built of stone and mud, and the interior was coated with a plaster mud to seal the cracks. Both the cliff stone houses and the stone houses in Tyuonyi were multi-storied and lacked windows and doors. Interior access was a hole in the roof via the ladder. Wood covered the entrance during cold or foul weather and at night. As a result, the interior was very dark. The lower levels of the stone houses were used primarily for storage. The upper rooms were only used for daily living during inclement weather or sleeping. The roof area was utilized during warmer months. Men would garden, hunt and weave. They would also travel to get or trade obsidian, hard lava glass. Or they would spend time working it with a bone tool, which would flake it off in extremely sharp pieces. Women would prepare food for storage or meals, maintain the household, care for children, and make pottery. The stone rooms that fronted the cliffs are now gone but the caves remain as a testimonial to those who came before. Soot from fires and the plaster mud linings still remain in some caves.

A word about food preparation and storage is imperative here. Gardening and food preparation took up most of the day. Corn on the cob was no larger than 4–5 inches. It was dried and then ground into "flour" for cooking. To grind it, the corn was smashed between two rocks resulting in a gritty flour. The grit would have sped up the wear on the teeth. The mere act of grinding the corn was very hard on the body and it could take up to half the day just to get enough flour for the day's meal. In addition to preparation, food storage was a critical part of the day. A great deal of food had to be stored properly for the community to make it through the winter, which was no small feat in a desert climate. In addition to the typical winter food storage, additional food storage was prepared. A Pueblo ideal was to have as much as five to seven years of food stored. A year with little rainfall may have been absorbed by the surpluses from the years before. However, successive years of drought must have caused a high degree of tension in an already difficult place to survive.

Creative approaches to living were necessities. Gardens were planted with mounded earth edges (much like a waffle) to capture rainfall and watchfully tended to ensure success. Cliff dwellings were constructed on the south-facing side of the canyon to take advantage of the winter sun. While *Tyuonyi* is in the middle on the bottom of the canyon with no south-facing advantage, most other large villages of the day were on the tops of mesas with cliff dwellings on the south-facing side of the mesa. The entryways into the cave dwellings were angled to avoid the hot summer sun and direct inward the low winter sun. The community continued to thrive for several more centuries in Frijoles Canyon.

Mother Nature can be cruel. By the middle of the 1500s, people had moved away from settlements throughout the Pajarito Plateau. Tree ring evidence shows a severe drought around the 1560s. Apparently the people didn't move very far. The people of Cochiti Pueblo, about thirty miles southwest along the Rio Grande, count the people from Frijoles Canyon among their ancestors.

Bandelier National Monument, named for Adolph F. A. Bandelier, consists of 32,000 acres containing more than 3,000 archeological sites that were homes of Ancestral Pueblo

Rock art! The soft "tuff" rock wore away from rain and running surface water forming alcoves. The alcoves are very cool in the summer and served as a refuge from the heat.

A close-up of the cliffs reveals the different colors of rock formed as the ash cooled. Erosion creates additional texture above the holes. Select holes were chosen to be enlarged for dwellings.

people. Bandelier was a self-taught archeologist with a keen interest in knowledge about the indigenous peoples in the Southwest. He traveled and studied the region speaking with the native people and asking questions about their ancestry. He was among the Cochiti Pueblo inquiring about ancestry when he first saw Frijoles Canyon. Apparently, he asked so many questions that they took him to their ancestral home in Frijoles Canyon, no easy hike in 1880. Despite the distance and terrain, upon arrival it immediately captivated Bandelier. He explored the area and, as a result, pioneered archeological and ethnographic studies in the southwest. His mappings and writings of the area and his fictional depiction of early Puebloan life prior to the Spaniards in *The Delight Makers*, published in 1890, intrigued other archeologists, most notably Edgar L. Hewett. Beginning in 1897, Hewett led several excavations of the dwellings in Frijoles Canyon. Both men's work led to the belief that history must be protected for the coming years as answers lay in the past. To this effect, Bandelier National Monument was created to preserve the ancestral Puebloan sites.

From the time the ancestral Pueblo people left until the early 1900s, Frijoles Canyon was never vacant. Spanish land grant holders were living in the area as well as Spanish shepherds who were grazing their sheep. In 1909, Frijoles Canyon again became a home to someone. Judge A. J. Abbott and his wife built a ranch and guest cabins in the canyon, calling it the Lodge of the Ten Elders. The area was designated as national monument in 1916. The Abbotts returned to Santa Fe in 1919.

Several other families had the lease to the ranch in the next few years, but 1925 brought more permanent settlers by the name of Evelyn and George Frey with their infant son, Richard. The Freys came to the Frijoles Canyon to manage the lodge for the Forest Service (it transferred to the National Park Service in 1932). The Freys tended an orchard, kept livestock and a garden and served huge home cooked meals for guests of the lodge.

At the time, Bandelier National Monument was a difficult place to visit, having an entrance trail only the most physically fit would attempt. It remained so until the 1930s when the Civilian Conservation Corp (C.C.C.) built a road and 31 buildings to facilitate tourism. Prior to the road, the trail managed to keep more people away than invite in. In the mid-1930s, The Lodge of the Ten Elders was removed, Mr. Frey left the area, the C.C.C. built a new lodge – the Frijoles Canyon Lodge, and Mrs. Frey stayed on to run it. She ran the lodge until she

The village of Tyuonyi lies on the Frijoles Canyon floor. It has been excavated and stabilized. If it were completely reconstructed, it would be multi-storied with ladders for access to the roofs. Access to the rooms would be through a hole in the roof and a ladder inside. Lower rooms served as storage for food. The upper rooms and roofs were homes and living space for people.

Evelyn Frey came to Bandelier in 1925 to manage the Lodge of the Ten Elders (above). She stayed until her death in 1988. *Courtesy of the National Park Service.*

closed the cabins for the last time in the fall of 1976. In 1978, she retired from the gift shop and worked the next ten years at the Visitor Center, until her death in September 1988. Remnants of her fruit trees still grace the landscape.

Today, in many ways, the Monument remains much as it did over 100 years ago when Adolph Bandelier first explored it. It still commands great respect for the people who lived there hundreds of years ago. Much of it remains untouched except for the effects of time and water. It still captivates the imagination and creates marvel at the strength and ingenuity of a group who could thrive in an area with a lifestyle so different from modern standards. Bandelier National Monument bears the name of the man who made it known to the world, and remains a lasting tribute to all who lived there throughout the centuries.

Opposite page: The landscape of Bandelier National Monument was formed by volcanic explosions 1.5 and 1.1 million years ago, and erosion in the intervening years. The rock is an excellent example of volcanic ash, known as tuff. The holes were made by erosion.

The Ancestral Pueblo people often built stone rooms in front of the cavates, or cave rooms. These rooms were reconstructed to allow today's visitor to fully comprehend how Frijoles Canyon was inhabited.

In the Tyuonyi village, small stone rooms were constructed. Their purpose was for winter grain storage and summer dispersal to the fields as well as living quarters. The rooms have been stabilized to give an idea of size and function. The architecture of Frijoles Canyon used local indigenous products. Pueblo people feel that a building has a life span - that it should be allowed to return to the earth once it is no longer used.

Rooms in the pueblo shared common walls and were stacked one on top of another. The lower ones were primarily storage while upper ones may have been living space for people who opted to live in Tyuonyi instead of the cliffs.

The *kiva,* or ceremonial room, was underground and had a roof. The *sipapu,* or spirit hole, is the small hole in the white stone in the middle of the floor. It symbolizes the people's place of origin and connection with the spirit world. A kiva is still the center of religious activites. It usually has a ventilator shaft, to bring in fresh air. The smoke escaped through the ladder hole in the roof.

The cliffs contain more than a thousand cavates, or cave rooms. There are several thousand unexcavated sites within the monument.

The Rito de los Frijoles or Little Bean Creek still flows today. It may have dried up as part of a drought in the 1500s forcing the occupants to leave Frijoles canyon in search of water. The holes in a line along the cliff were carved into the stone to anchor roof and floor beams.

The cave houses are only on the south-facing side of the cliffs situated to take advantage of any warmth from the winter sun.

Inside the cave, there is sometimes a niche carved in the wall for storage. The ceiling is usually black from fires used for heating and cooking.

Bibliography

Kantner, John. "Sipapu-Frequently Asked Questions." [http://sipapu.gsu.edu/html/faq.html]. 12/6/04

National Park Service. "Bandelier." [http://www.nps.gov/band]. 12/6/04

Desert USA. "The Anasazi." [http://www.desertusa.com/ind1/du_peo_ana.html]. 12/6/04

Desert USA. "Bandelier National Monument Description." [http://www.desertusa.com/ban/du_bandesc.html]. 12/6/04

Bureau of Land Management, Colorado. "The Ancestral Pueblos (Anasazi)." [http://www.co.blm.gov/ahc/anasazi.htm]. 12/6/04

No Author. "5/24/1929 – Judge A. J. Abbott, distinguished old timer, dies here at age 87." [http://users.ipfw.edu/abbott/family/AJABBOTTObit.htm]. 12/3/06

Western National Parks Association. "Bandelier - Mrs. Frey's stories." [http://www.wnpa.org/freepubs/band/freystories.pdf]. 12/7/04

Office of Senator Jeff Bingaman. "Projects of the Civilian Conservation Corps-Bandelier National Monument." [http://Bingaman.senate.gov/New_Mexico/projects.html]. 12/5/04

Harrison, Laura Soullière. Architecture in the Parks – "Bandelier National Monument CCC Historic District. (online book). [http://www.cr.nps.gov/history/online_books/Harrison/harrison23.htm]. 12/6/04

Other References

Great Southwest Adventures
Monique Schoustra
P. O. Box 31151
Santa Fe, NM 87594-1151
(505) 455-2700

Today, the viewer is left to wonder how to reach the cave dwellings high in the cliffs. The ancients probably built stone structures into the cliffs before they reached the caves. The small circular holes are from timber roofs, the small rectangles are storage niches, and the large openings are cave home entrances. Below: This cave has three rooms connected on the inside and all accessible from outside. The small hole above the laddered entrance may have been an existing hole from the volcanic activity or created to vent a fire.

Holes in the rocks created natural ladders and access to create petroglyphs (stone drawings). The physique of the ancients was short with a stocky build – perfect for rock climbing. Right: A cholla, or jumping cactus, provides scale for the cliffs and stone room. The stone rooms are also called talus houses as they were constructed on talus, or rock debris, slopes.

A painted design, or pictograph, remains next to the entrance to a cave home while the timbers and stone room in front of the cave are gone. Only pictographs located in protected locations, such as this alcove, remain; this one has been covered with glass to prevent damage by people and weather. Petroglyphs, drawings carved into stone, are also vulnerable to erosion and disrespectful people.